VASILY KANDINSKY

ediciones polígrafa

masterpieces
VASILY KANDINSKY

© 2005 Ediciones Polígrafa, S.A.
Balmes, 54. E-08007 Barcelona
www.edicionespoligrafa.com

Reproductions copyright © Vasily Kandinsky, VEGAP, Barcelona 2005
© Text: José María Faerna
Translation: Alberto Curotto (biography: Sue Brownbridge)
Color separation: Format Digital (Barcelona)
Printed and bound at Mateu Cromo (Madrid)

Available in USA and Canada through D.A.P./Distributed Art Publishers
155 Sixth Avenue, 2nd Floor, New York, N.Y. 10013
Tel: (212) 627–1999 Fax: (212) 627–9484

ISBN: 84-343-1074-0
Dep. legal: B. 34.604 - 2005 (Printed in Spain)

CONTENTS

7 KANDINSKY AND ABSTRACTION

11 VASILY KANDINSKY, 1866–1944

16 SELECTED BIOGRAPHY

18 FORMATIVE INFLUENCES

25 DEVELOPMENTS IN MUNICH

31 ABANDONING REPRESENTATION

41 NON-OBJECTIVE PAINTING

52 THE FOLKLORIC IMAGINATION

56 A MORE RIGOROUS STYLE

60 POINT AND LINE TO PLANE

66 A NEW FREEDOM

78 LIST OF WORKS

KANDINSKY AND ABSTRACTION

Vasily Kandinsky is considered the founder of abstract painting, and any assessment of his importance in the history of modern art must give an account of how that central innovation came about. As often happens with "breakthrough" developments, however, the chronology of specific events is open to debate. For example, most scholars now believe that the small watercolor which is often considered the first abstract (or "non-objective") composition—dated 1910 by Kandinsky—was actually made somewhat later than that. Moreover, there exist a number of isolated examples of nonrepresentational paintings by other artists from before World War I, some as early as 1910. But that is exactly what they are: isolated examples, not the heralds of a radically new aesthetic. For despite the complexities of chronology, it remains clear that Kandinsky was the first painter to "abstract" from the appearance of the objects of the world in a truly programmatic manner—the first to view the renunciation of the representational as a necessary step toward a purer kind of painting.

VARIETIES OF ABSTRACTION

Kandinsky was the principal innovator of abstraction, yet it is important to note that not all modern abstract art can be traced to him. His project was related to other avant-garde movements that emerged in the early decades of the century —Constructivism, Suprematism, Neoplasticism—which also practiced nonrepresentational painting, but often those groups pursued such experiments as part of a larger program, aimed at transforming modern society as well as the visual arts. Nor did the

great current of abstraction that dominated modern art between
1945 and 1965, especially in the United States, issue directly
from Kandinsky. Indeed, the primary inspiration for artists such as
Jackson Pollock, Mark Rothko, Willem de Kooning, or, in Europe,
Karel Appel, came not from the first abstract painters at all, but
rather from such movements as Surrealism and Cubism, which had,
in fact, refused to make the leap into the non-objective.

This, however, does not diminish Kandinsky's crucial role in the
development of modern art. Although not all the varieties of abstract
art descend directly from his work, his precedent made them
possible. He made it legitimate to sever all ties to the "motif"—the
depicted subject—and thereby freed the artist to concentrate on the
paint itself, and on how its manipulation in lines, shapes, and forms
affected the viewer. To liberate the elements of painting in this
way has been one of the great aspirations of modern art, not only
since Henri Matisse and Pablo Picasso, but since the time of the
Impressionists. It was, in fact, the experience of seeing a work by
Claude Monet that profoundly influenced the young Kandinsky and
won him over to the cause of modern painting.

THE SPIRITUAL IN ART

Though Kandinsky's mature work does not seek to imitate the
appearance of the physical world, neither does it limit itself to mere
decoration. Abstract art was not conceived as a way to produce
pretty patterns for their own sake, but as a way to communicate
more directly with the soul of the viewer. Kandinsky's art disregards
the material world in order to attend more closely to the spiritual

one. As with a musical composition, the arrangement of colors in one of his abstract paintings is guided solely by the principles of harmony and contrast, with the intention that this particular combination of elements will strike a resonant chord within the spectator. Kandinsky was in this regard following in the steps of the German and Northern European Romantic tradition, according to which the underlying subject matter of art, despite its many varied material forme, is always the unchanging world of the spirit.

SYNESTHESIA

For Kandinsky, the comparison of painting with music was more than simply a metaphor. An awareness of his profound interest in music is crucial to any understanding of his work. The use of musical terms in the titles of his paintings, such as the groups called Improvisations or Compositions, is not gratuitous: instead, it conforms to the notion of "synesthesia," the idea that there are interconnections between the different bodily senses, such as hearing and vision, whereby colors are associated with specific sounds and musical harmonies on the one hand, and with particular emotional states on the other.

Kandinsky wrote about such phenomena in *On the Spiritual in Art* (1911), a brief treatise that defines the equivalencies between colors and concepts that are the basis of his painting. Spiritualistic ideas, derived from theosophy and occultism, also played an important role in reinforcing his ideas about sound and vision. But most of all, Kandinsky's understanding of the connection between painting and music derived from the Romantic operas of Richard Wagner. With his unusual interest in coordinating the effects of scenery and stage

lighting with the performance of the score, Wagner conceived of his music dramas as a "total" aesthetic experience, one in which the visual and the auditory components would coalesce into a single, unified experience that would deeply affect the viewer's innermost being. As a result of Wagner's widespread irfluence, the notion of synesthesia became important for many artists, composers, and poets in the late nineteenth and early twentieth centuries.

THE AIMS OF ART

Possibly because of his academic background, Kandinsky always had a penchant for theory, which led him to try to systematize his thinking about the ultimate goals of art through a number of discursive writings. Moreover, the awareness that he was establishing a new kind of painting increased his need to develop an intellectual rationale for his work. His years as a professor at the Bauhaus—the German school that in the 1920s and 1930s tried to apply the ideas of the avant-garde to architecture and industrial design—witnessed an even more thorough systemization of his theory of painting, notably in the volume *Point and Line to Plane* (1926), a sort of textbook for his classes. His more rigorous way of thinking at that time was not unrelated to the ideas of his Bauhaus colleague Josef Albers concerning the interactions of colors, and Kandinsky's work as an artist also became more disciplined in those years, pursuing a rigorously geometric style. Yet Kandinsky continued to seek the final significance of his paintings in the musical and emotional qualities that he ascribed to color. "Color," he said, "is the medium by which one can affect the soul directly. . . . The soul is a piano with many strings, and the artist is the hand that, by striking one particular key, causes the human soul to vibrate."

Kandinsky executed this drawing in India ink for the cover of the catalogue of the first Blue Rider exhibition, in 1911, a year before the publication of the famous almanac *The Blue Rider*.

LITTLE WORLDS VI, 1922. Kandinsky re-created the world of his paintings in graphic works such as this.

In this, Kandinsky strove to fulfill the old aspiration of the Romantic movement for a "total" art, one capable of transforming how we understand the world around us. Therefore, his aims were indeed related to the larger project shared by much of the twentieth-century avant-garde—to rejuvenate a broad range of human endeavor, beginning with the visual arts. Kandinsky's utopia, however, was neither social nor political, but spiritual. His ultimate goal was to facilitate what he called the "inner gaze," that is, a personal vision revealing the hidden soul of things.

VASILY KANDINSKY, 1866-1944

Kandinsky was born in Moscow of a well-to-do family, and although he spent most of his life in Germany and France, he always retained strong emotional ties to his homeland and its culture. During the first thirty years of his life, in Russia, painting remained only a kind of passionate diversion for this seemingly conventional young man, who was actually of a deeply Romantic disposition. After he completed his studies in law, his brilliant academic record earned him a professional position, but he gave it up in 1896 to move to Munich and devote himself entirely to painting.

THE EARLY YEARS IN MUNICH

The Bavarian capital, where the style known as Jugendstil was developing, was one of Europe's busiest artistic centers. Kandinsky studied painting at the Munich Academy and met Alexei von Jawlensky and Paul Klee, two of the artists with whom he would

be closely associated. He also met the painter Gabriele Münter (see p. 29). The intense relationship between them, which lasted from 1902 until 1914, precipitated Kandinsky's separation from his first wife.

Kandinsky in Dresden, 1905. This was a productive period in the artist's life. In 1906, he would travel with Münter to Paris, where he remained until the next year.

In Munich, Kandinsky organized a number of artists' associations designed to promote exhibitions. Phalanx, the first of these groups, was founded in 1901 and showed works by the Impressionists and the Symbolists, artists who had a visible irfluence on Kandinsky's early paintings. In the same years, Kandinsky began experimenting with woodcuts, a medium with a tradition in Germany going back to the Middle Ages.

DEVELOPING A PERSONAL STYLE

During 1906–8, Kandinsky traveled in Europe with Münter, exhibited at the Salon d'Automne and the Salon des Indépendants in Paris, and saw works by the Fauvists and the emerging Cubists. The irfluence of Fauve color can be seen in the works that he painted in 1908 and 1909 after settling in the German city of Murnau. At that time, with Alfred Kubin, Jawlensky, Münter, and others he founded the New Coalition of Munich Artists—known by its German acronym, NKVM. The ideas that would give rise to abstraction were beginning to form: in particular, Kandinsky pursued his interests in theosophy and occultism through the writings of Rudolf Steiner and Madame Blavatsky, which were extremely popular in European cultural circles at the time.

This period also marked the beginning of his friendship with the pioneer of atonal musical composition, Arnold Schoenberg.

Maria and Franz Marc, Bernhard
Koehler (père), Heinrich
Campendonk, Thomas von Hartmann,
and Kandinsky (seated), 1911.

Kandinsky with his son, Vsevdod,
in Moscow, 1918.

Schoenberg's development of a kind of music liberated from
traditional harmony may have contributed to Kandinsky's
development of a kind of painting freed from traditional
representation. The composer may also have encouraged
Kandinsky's thinking about synesthesia and the interconnections
between music and painting.

During this time, the NKVM exhibitions presented works by
some of the most important of the Parisian painters, including
Picasso, André Derain, Georges Braque, and Maurice de Vlaminck.
Kandinsky's work of the time, however, such as the study for
Composition II (p. 33), still had not let go of the conventions
of representational painting, although, in a manner somewhat
related to Fauvism, its subjects were beginning to dissolve into a
vortex of colored shapes. Such works exemplify the ambiguous,
transitional stage through which his art was passing at that
point.

EXPLORING AN ABSTRACT WORLD

Even this partial dismantling of representation was not welcomed
by the NKVM. Kandinsky, however, continued to look toward greater
abstraction, writing his treatise *On the Spiritual in Art,* published
in 1911. In 1912, with Jawlensky and Münter, he left the NKVM
and founded his last and best-known Munich group, the Blue
Rider. In the process, Kandinsky met Franz Marc, with whom he
collaborated both in the group's exhibitions and in the publication
of an almanac, in which they expounded their theoretical principles
and commented on the art that aroused their interest, from the work

of such contemporaries as Picasso and Derain, to African art, to the Russian and German folk traditions. Among the other artists who exhibited with the Blue Rider were August Macke, Schoenberg, and the Parisian painter Robert Delaunay. Kandinsky was by this time working in a truly abstract mode.

At the outbreak of World War I in 1914, Kandinsky returned to Russia. There, the great upheaval surrounding the October Revolution of 1917 was also a time of artistic ferment, with the participation of some of the most advanced artistic movements of the twentieth century. Although his spirituality and his Romanticism were at odds with the prevailing materialism of the government and most of the leading Russian artists, Kandinsky held a number of important artistic and cultural offices in the administration of the new Soviet state. His efforts led to the founding of several museums throughout Russia and to the development of new educational programs.
In 1917, Kandinsky married Nina Adreevsky, his second wife.
Four years later, the two left for Berlin, and Kandinsky never again returned to Russia.

From Walter Gropius came the offer of a position at the Bauhaus, where Kandinsky led both the Decorative Painting Workshop and the introductory course from 1922 to 1933. At the Bauhaus, he found his old friend Klee, and with him Jawlensky and Lyonel Feininger. During those years, Kandinsky's work became more rigorous in composition. His devotion to color was supplemented by a new appreciation for geometry and by a more controlled interaction of forms, as his painting responded to the various stylistic currents at the Bauhaus.

LATER YEARS

With the closing of the Bauhaus by the Nazis in 1933, Kandinsky was forced to leave Germany—his paintings would be among those included in the exhibition of condemned works called "Degenerate Art" in 1937— and he settled in Neuilly, near Paris. There he hoped to find a climate favorable to his work, but the French artistic scene was not at that time especially well disposed toward abstraction. André Breton unsuccessfully tried to win him over to the Surrealist cause and, although Kandinsky became a French citizen, the last phase of his career unfolded quietly, amid a general lack of critical understanding of his work. In his last paintings, Kandinsky drifted away from Bauhaus geometry and used more organic and biomorphic shapes. He died in 1944, too soon to witness the triumph of abstract art in the postwar era.

1866 Wassily Kandinsky is born on 4 December in Moscow.

1871 The family, originally from western Siberia on his father's side, settles in Odessa, where he goes to school. He studies music (the cello and piano).

1886 He studies law and economics in Moscow. The mystical beauty of the city and its icons make a profound impression on him.

1889 The Society of Natural Sciences, Ethnography and Anthropology sends him on a mission to the far north-east. He publishes articles on ethnography and law. The rich folklore of ancient Russia greatly influences him. On his first visit to an *izba*, a Russian log house, he comments that he felt as if he were "entering into painting".
He makes his first trip to Paris and returns to the French capital in 1892.

1893 He teaches at the Faculty of Law in Moscow.

1896 He gives up teaching law and decides to devote himself entirely to painting. He goes to Munich.

1897 He studies under Anton Azbé.

1900 He studies alongside Paul Klee under Franz von Stück, who does not approve of his "extravagances with color."

1900 He founds the association Phalanx with a number of other painters. Phalanx organizes exhibitions and courses in painting with a view to raising the public's awareness of the "art of tomorrow", and also calls into question traditional academic training. Kandinsky, among others, advocates sending his students to visit churches in Bavaria.

1902 He shows work in the exhibition of the Berlin Sezession, which he is a member of. He meets the painter Gabriele Münter, whom he lives with until 1916.

1903 On his return to Moscow, he publishes his woodcuts *Poems without Words*.

1904 He travels to Paris, where he shows work in the Salon d'Automne, and then goes on to Tunis.

1905 He lives in Italy for a year with Gabriele Münter.

1906 He lives in Paris for two years with Münter. He then spends two years in Sèvres.

1908 On his return to Munich, he envisages his first staged works with the help of the composer Thomas von Hartmann and the dancer Alexandre Sacharoff.

1909 He founds the Neue Künstlervereinigung (New Artists Association). He shows work in the exhibition of graphic art organized in Dresden by the Die Brücke group. He publishes an album of woodcuts in Paris.

1910 He plays an active role in numerous exhibitions, in particular in Russia.
He turns increasingly to watercolor as his preferred experimental technique.

1911 He and Franz Marc found Der Blaue Reiter (The Blue Rider), which puts on an exhibition in December. *On the Spiritual in Art*, which gives an explanation of his aesthetic philosophy, is published.

1912 *Der Blaue Reiter Almanac* is published. He has his first solo exhibition at the Galerie Der Sturm in Berlin, which unfailingly supports him for several years.

1913 He publishes *Klänge* (Sounds) in Munich and *Reminiscences* in Berlin.

1914 He is forced by the war to move to Switzerland, where he remains from August to November, when he makes his way back to Russia via Italy and the Balkans.

1915 He spends some time in Stockholm for a solo exhibition.

1917 The October Revolution.

1918 He becomes a professor at State Free Art Studios Higher Art and Technical Studios and is charged with setting up and reorganizing the museums of the Soviet Union. Twenty-two museums are organized under his direction.
He meets Chagall, Pevsner and Gabo.

1920 Official exhibition in Moscow organized by the state.

1921 Kandinsky is made deputy director of the Russian Academy of Artistic Sciences in Moscow.
He receives an invitation from the Bauhaus in Weimar and decides to move there.

1922 After spending some time in Berlin, he takes up his post as a professor at the Bauhaus. His main friends there are Paul Klee and Lyonel Feininger.
He creates vast wall paintings for all the walls in one of the rooms in the Juryfreie Kunstausstellung.

1925 The Bauhaus is severely criticized by the National Socialists and moves to Dessau.

1926 The Bauhaus publishes Kandinsky's essay *Point and Line to Plane*.

An exhibition is held at the Galerie Arnold in Dresden to celebrate Kandinsky's 60th birthday. The preface to the accompanying catalogue is written by Paul Klee. Other events are also held in Dessau and Berlin to mark the occasion.

1928 Kandinsky designs the sets and costumes for Mussorgsky's *Pictures at an Exhibition*.

1929 He travels to Belgium, where he meets Ensor. His first exhibition in Paris. Marcel Duchamp pays him a visit at the Bauhaus.

1930 He shows work in the exhibition of the Cercle et Carré group, the immediate predecessor of the Abstraction-Création group, which in turn folds in 1936.

1931 He designs ceramic tile murals in the music room designed by Mies van der Rohe for the International Architecture Exhibition in Berlin.

1932 The Bauhaus is closed by order of the National Socialists and moves to Berlin, where it continues to exist as a private school.

1933 Under threat from the Gestapo, the Bauhaus closes. Kandinsky moves to Paris.

1934 Now settled in Neuilly-sur-Seine and sustained by the friendship of the Surrealists, he continues to paint and exhibit work. He meets Miró, Mondrian, Delaunay and Magnelli.

1937 At the same time as the Kunsthalle in Berne is presenting a retrospective of his work, the Nazis seize some 50 of his canvases in German museums on the grounds that they are "degenerate art" and sell them abroad.

1939 Kandinsky and his wife Nina are granted French citizenship. The war breaks out not long afterwards.

1940 He flees to the Pyrenees but then returns to Paris for the duration of the war.

1941 Kandinsky is twice invited by the United States to go there but refuses to leave Paris.

1944 He exhibits with Domela and Nicolas de Staël.
He falls ill in March and does not paint again. He dies on 13 December.

FORMATIVE INFLUENCES

Two events that shaped Kandinsky's artistic vocation took place in 1895: he attended a performance of Richard Wagner's opera *Lohengrin,* and he saw one of Claude Monet's Haystack paintings at an exhibition of Impressionist art in Moscow. Kandinsky's response to Wagner at this early date already points to the link between painting and music that would inform his work as an artist. And his response to Monet indicates something of his future course toward nonrepresentational painting, for it was precisely the dematerializing of the motif in Monet's painting, the way that objects were beginning to dissolve into color and light, that impressed Kandinsky, who was captivated by the work. "Unknowingly," he wrote many years later, "the inevitability of the object as a pictorial element was being discredited." Not surprisingly, then, his first painted works reveal the influence of Impressionist color, as later on he would be affected by the color experiments of the Fauves. In Paris in 1906–7, Kandinsky was able to expand his knowledge of many of the French artists, including those who had participated in the Phalanx exhibitions from 1901 to 1904—Monet, Paul Signac, Félix Vallotton, Henri de Toulouse-Lautrec—and those who would participate in the exhibitions of the NKVM: Picasso, Braque, Vlaminck, André Derain, Kees van Dongen, Henri Le Fauconnier, and Georges Rouault.

THE OLD CITY II, 1902. The mellow evening light gives a poetic aura to this view of Rothenburg, but the sharp, clear-cut volumes recall Paul Cézanne's paintings. Kandinsky's minute brushstrokes, heavy with pigment, make tiny tesserae of color. They suggest the perfectionist preciosity typical of many painters of that period, from Lovis Corinth to Gustav Klimt.

KOCHEL: WATERFALL I, 1900. The notion that a landscape betrays
"the state of the soul" dates from Romanticism. Kandinsky may have
been influenced by nineteenth-century Russian painting or by the
landscapists of the Barbizon school. But more than these, the
immediacy of this canvas, with its generous brushstrokes, reveals
the influence of the late Impressionist manner that had left its
mark on the painter at a Moscow exhibition in 1895.

RIEGSEE: THE TOWN CHURCH,1908.
The arbitrariness of Fauve color
is one of the most important
innovations that Kandinsky
incorporated into his own
painterly style upon his return
to Germany from France in 1908.
By emancipating color from the
restraints of fidelity to
nature, he took the first step
toward pictorial autonomy—toward
painting as a chromatic
symphony.

MUNICH: SCHWABING WITH
THE CHURCH OF ST. URSULA, 1908.
Another striking example of
the effect on Kandinsky of his
encounter with Fauvism.

LANDSCAPE WITH A TOWER, 1908. In this mysterious nocturnal setting, the pervasive red-yellow color chord of the brick tower, the roofs, and the field in the lower left corner takes on a somewhat spectral character.

INTERIOR (MY DINING ROOM), 1909. The influence of Félix Vallotton, whose works were shown at the tenth Phalanx exhibition in 1910, as well as that of the French Nabi artists, can be seen in this meticulously painted, decorative interior.

MOUNTAIN, 1909. The narrative
element is downplayed in favor
of a pure harmony of colors.
Yellow, red, blue, and green—the
basis of Kandinsky's chromatic
vocabulary—here create a feeling
of ascent, as he arranges the
color areas with the brighter,
lighter hues toward the top of
the painting.

DEVELOPMENTS IN MUNICH

OBERMARKT WITH MOUNTAINS, 1908. This is one of the earliest works painted in the small Bavarian village where Kandinsky sojourned with Gabriele Münter. The pale yet luminous color confers an air of melancholy on the scene, which is treated with the sharp contrast of light and shade typical of woodcuts. The picture's style may also owe something to Ferdinand Hodler.

In 1896, at the time of Kandinsky's arrival in Munich, the Bavarian capital was one of Europe's most important modernist centers. In 1892, a group of artists had broken away from the official academy and founded the Secession movement, which included some of the foremost painters of that time, such as Lovis Corinth and Franz von Stuck. The same year saw the first publication of the review *Jugend*, from which the German modernist style called Jugendstil took its name, and whose orbit attracted such figures as Hermann Obrist and August Endell. Their irfluence is evident in several of Kandinsky's works, such as his poster for the Phalanx exhibitions, but his strongest link to the Munich art world was his devotion to Romantic idealism, which had already emerged while he was in Russia. Kandinsky assimilated the melancholic tone of Symbolism, one of the prevailing currents of the Secession, and its taste for landscape. The inner correspondence of color with the emotions is part of this Romantic heritage, which Kandinsky combined with the irfluence of Fauvism.

THE BLUE RIDER, 1903. At this very early date, Kandinsky introduced
what would become the emblem of the most famous of the several
groups that he belonged to in his career. For the artist, blue was
a celestial symbol; he equated this spiritual rider with the
mythical St. George, defeating the "dragon" of materialism. His
mysterious presence in the landscape, bathed in an eerie raking
light, evokes the atmosphere of German folktales.

RIDING COUPLE, 1906-7. The ornamental quality of Kandinsky's early pointillism makes it not unlike the work of Gustav Klimt, and, like that Viennese artist, Kandinsky here explores the decorative aspects of painting as they relate to architectural design. Though the subject suggests a Russian folktale, it is depicted against the transfigured silhouette of an imaginary Moscow—a magical skyline of gilded domes—on the opposite bank of the river.

THE FAREWELL, 1903. During his
first years in Munich, Kandinsky
produced more woodcuts than oil
paintings. This printmaking
technique had been deeply rooted
in German tradition since the
late Middle Ages, and at the
beginning of the twentieth
century it was revived by
artists of many different
persuasions. Both the legendary
subject of this work and
Kandinsky's linear and
decorative draftsmanship are
clearly related to the woodcut
tradition.

PORTRAIT OF GABRIELE MÜNTER, 1905. The Phalanx group operated an
art school, where Kandinsky met Gabriele Münter, a young German
painter who shared his life until 1914. In Moscow, Kandinsky had
been married to his cousin, Anna Chemiakina, from whom he was
amicably divorced in 1911, when his relationship with Münter was
already long established. Münter's sensitive, intelligent features
appear in several portraits that Kandinsky painted in those years.

BLUE MOUNTAIN, 1908-9. This image of horseback riders before a
towering blue mountain—a color symbolizing the spiritual—is clearly
allegorical. The blue-red-yellow triad constitutes one of the basic
chromatic harmonies of Kandinsky's work in these years.

ABANDONING REPRESENTATION

The period from 1908 to 1910 was a personally rewarding one for
Kandinsky, as reflected in the remarkable artistic progress of those
years. With Gabriele Münter, he bought a house in Murnau, where he
was able to spend long periods painting. Until at least 1912,
recognizable objects continued to appear in some of his works, but
the move to abstraction had already been made. The motif was
increasingly dissolved into expanses of color, although he said that as
yet he dared not discard it entirely for fear of falling into a merely
decorative mode, or producing paintings "that resemble, to say it
crudely, carpets or neckties. The beauty of color and form is not
enough of a goal for art." He therefore sought to endow painting with
spiritual values comparable to those he found in music. It was then
that Kandinsky began calling his works Improvisations and
Compositions, as though they were musical pieces.

MURNAU: VIEW WITH RAILROAD AND
CASTLE, 1909. The flattening
of depicted objects, turning
them into silhouettes, recalls
the woodcuts that Kandinsky
made during his first years in
Munich.

Sketch for COMPOSITION II, 1910. The final version of this work,
Kandinsky's most ambitious up to that time, was lost in World War II.
Shortly after its completion, it was shown at the second NKVM
exhibition, where it aroused controversy. The welter of seemingly
unrelated figures, caught in a whirlpool of color, signals a
crucial stage in the painter's artistic development, the beginning
of the break with representation.

IMPROVISATION VI, 1909.
Kandinsky had visited Tunis
with Gabriele Münter, and echoes
of that trip can be found in
some works from the time. The
subtitle "Africana" is sometimes
affixed to this painting, in
which Kandinsky incorporated his
experience of North Africa into
his quest for a new artistic
idiom.

IMPROVISATION VII, 1910.
Along with COMPOSITION II
(see study, p. 33), this is
one of the earliest paintings
in which Kandinsky discarded
representation. The color
arrangement, with barely any
delimiting linear structure,
transforms pictorial space into a
zone of chromatic turbulence,
a vortex that spirals in to the
upper right quadrant of the
painting.

IMPROVISATION XVIII (WITH
TOMBSTONES), 1911. The absence
of hierarchical order in this
painting is characteristic of
the works of 1910 and 1911, as
Kandinsky explored new
territory.

PASSAGE BY BOAT, 1910. The subject of a boat with oarsmen appears frequently in these years, a time when Kandinsky thought of pure abstraction as a "voyage" to the terra incognita of a new world of painting. The oarsmen steer toward unknown waters, as the artist does; like him, they voyage from darkness to light.

IMPROVISATION XIX, 1911. The discontinuity between the figures, who
are rendered with rough black brushstrokes, and the background of
the painting—a broad, mottled area of variations on blue, and a
warm, red border with touches of yellow and green— makes it
possible to speak of color and line as two independent, almost
unrelated structures. The harmony of the colors would be just as
intelligible without the representational sketch: the insubstantial
figures are hardly more than a way to emphasize the tension at the
edges of the painting.

ALL SAINTS' DAY I, 1911. The same year, Kandinsky completed a representational version of this painting using a similar chromatic arrangement. In the present version, the areas of color intermingle in a maelstrom of directional tensions that establishes no clear hierarchical order.

AUTUMN II, 1912. The tenuous
diagonal across the lower
portion of the painting gives
rise to a spectacular image:
a diaphanous landscape of soft,
autumn hues is reflected in
the still waters of a lake.
In this case, it is the title
that provides the key to the
painting's colors, as elsewhere
it is given by a reference to
music.

NON-OBJECTIVE PAINTING

COMPOSITION IV, 1911. The rainbow that arches between the mountains establishes the basic color harmony, a blue, yellow, and green chord with strokes of red. The black lines are little more than a template laid over the areas of color.

During the years from 1910 to the outbreak of World War I, Kandinsky created his own painterly domain. The openly nonrepresentational nature of his work caused tensions with the NKVM, which in 1911 refused to exhibit his *Composition* V (private collection), claiming that its format did not comply with the mandatory requirements of the association. But as a result, Kandinsky strengthened his friendships with Franz Marc and Arnold Schoenberg, which led to the forming of the Blue Rider. At the same time, Kandinsky pursued his interest in theosophy, which was to become a spiritual resource for his work as an artist. His paintings were already nonrepresentational; only a few spare brushstrokes occasionally still hinted at figures and objects, now more as oblique allusions to the painting's meaning than as its actual subject. Such vestiges of representation only served to demonstrate Kandinsky's awareness of his role as the founder of a new kind of painting: with their traces of such subjects as the Deluge, the Apocalypse, and the voyage to unknown waters, these works are all images of a great ending, but also of regeneration and of arrival in a new, reborn world. The theme of these paintings is not merely the conflict between vibrant masses of color but, as the artist said, "the perception of the spiritual in material and abstract things."

IMPROVISATION XIII, 1910.
Paintings like this one, in
which representational content
has dissolved into color, best
exemplify Kandinsky's work
during the years before World
War I. Here, the masses of
color are contained by thick
black strokes that might as
well be cast shadows.

ST. GEORGE II, 1911. Differently
colored angular shapes cluster
like vectors around a yellow
diagonal. The organization of
the painting is reminiscent of
certain Cubist ideas of spatial
structure; however, both the
date of this work and the
nature of Kandinsky's aesthetic
decisions make it diffcult to
imagine a direct influence.

DELUGE I, 1912. Kandinsky's
allusion to the biblical Deluge
is one of the most frequent
metaphors of regeneration at
this stage of his career. Here,
a downpour of shapes tumbles
through a range of colors, from
the intense yellows to white to
the reddish-greens at the back.

IMPROVISATION (DELUGE), 1913. Once again, Kandinsky alludes to the biblical Deluge and to the idea of chaos. Here, however, the relatively cool colors and the black background dampen the explosive energy of the scene, and Kandinsky lowers the temperature of the large red shapes by putting layers of calmer colors on top of them. The three rays across the upper part of the painting suggest the symbolic oars in the works that he painted in 1910 (see p. 37).

Study for DELUGE II, 1912. The entire composition responds to
the diagonal current that originates in the lower left corner.
The warmest and most vibrant tones—yellows and reds—create the
foreground, with blues and browns for the most part restricted to
the top and right.

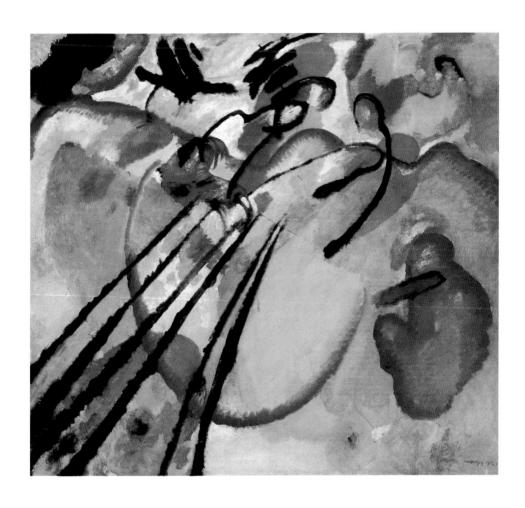

IMPROVISATION XXVI (ROWING), 1912. A wavy red line splits the
pictorial surface into two unequal parts. Once again, rowing figures
are defined by a few black strokes, here laid over the pattern of
color areas. The black lines establish a forceful diagonal that
gives the painting its dynamic quality, and they thus impose a
certain tension on the more static background. By showing the
tension between such wholly different elements, Kandinsky wanted to
convey the opposition between the material and spiritual worlds.

COMPOSITION VI, 1913. Kandinsky
called his most complex
paintings Compositions, and
each was generally preceded by
a number of preliminary studies.
Works such as this are among
his most intricate pictorial
structures and can scarcely be
appreciated in reproduction.

FANTASTIC IMPROVISATION, 1913.
The dark blot at the center
of the painting draws the swirl-
ing strokes of color into one
central vortex of movement.
The more isolated areas in the
corners act as a frame for
this dominant motion.

MOSCOW II, 1916. This painting was executed after Kandinsky's return to Russia at the outbreak of World War I. It is illuminating to compare it with his written description of sunset in his native city: "The sun dissolves the whole of Moscow into a single spot, which ... sets all of one's soul vibrating.... It is the last chord of the symphony, which brings every color vividly to life, which allows, even forces, all of Moscow to resound like the final fortissimo of a gigantic orchestra.... To paint this hour, I thought, must be for an artist the most impossible, the greatest joy."

BLACK LINES I, 1913. The expansiveness that Kandinsky attributed to the color yellow is here offset by the compact density of the reds and blues, which, with their greater compositional "weight," slip toward the bottom. The graphic lines in the work do not conflict with this underlying painted structure, but instead complement it, giving the viewer a schematic means of reading the picture. With each painting, Kandinsky tested anew the relationship between color and line.

THE FOLKLORIC IMAGINATION

During the greater part of his childhood in Russia, Kandinsky was raised by his aunt, Elisabeth Ticheeva, who used to read him Russian and German folktales. In 1889, the Society of Natural Sciences, Ethnography, and Anthropology invited him on a scientific mission to Vologda, in northern Russia, to study agrarian law as well as the surviving traces of pre-Christian religions in the area. These circumstances attest to Kandinsky's early interest in folklore and indigenous culture, among the constants in the Romantic tradition of Northern Europe. In Munich, Kandinsky continued to follow this particular predilection and, as a result, several paintings from his early years depict Russian and German legends and popular figures. It is worth noting his profound interest in the specifically Bavarian tradition, dating from the eighteenth and nineteenth centuries, of depicting naïve, vignette-like religious scenes in the medium of small votive paintings on glass. The almanac published by the Blue Rider in 1912 reproduced works of this kind from the Krötz collection, as well as a series of popular prints of various cultural origins. What Kandinsky looked for in these sources were signs of a spirituality still uncontaminated by subsequent cultural developments. Kandinsky himself, who never forgot the icons of his native Russia, made paintings on glass as well as woodcuts in the old German tradition.

SONG OF THE VOLGA, 1906. The painter evokes the atmosphere of the Russian folktales of his childhood and the decorative sensibility typical of the German Jugendstil. Although he lingers over such ornamental features as the icons on the masts or the boats' carved figureheads, the whole scene is nonetheless rendered in a vigorous manner.

GLASS PAINTING WITH SUN, 1910. Bavarian paintings on glass may have put Kandinsky in mind of Russian icons. The idea of painting the frame, however, belongs to a modern tradition according to which a work of art should be a decorative synthesis.

LAST JUDGMENT, 1912. Apocalyptic imagery recurs frequently in this
period of transition toward an abstract art. In this work, both the
medium of painting on glass and the decorative treatment of the
frame suggest ties to folk culture.

WOMAN IN MOSCOW, 1912. Only rarely did Kandinsky return to figurative art, and when he did it was almost always to deal with memories of his childhood in Russia. The frontal rendition of the central figure here may have been suggested by Russian icons, while the general atmosphere, with mysterious characters floating in midair, is not unlike the fables painted by his countryman Marc Chagall. The choice of colors is quite typical of Kandinsky's other work in those years.

A MORE RIGOROUS STYLE

The years that Kandinsky spent in Russia before again going to
Germany, to join the Bauhaus in 1921, were not very productive in
terms of the number of works he made. He was kept busy by his
responsibilities in the cultural and artistic administration of the
new state that had issued from the Revolution. Nonetheless, the
paintings that he produced in this period display some significant
developments. In spite of his differences with the leading factions of
the Russian avant-garde, the influence of their work is clearly felt in
the process of systematic analysis that now overtook the flowing
chromaticism of the Blue Rider period. Kandinsky wanted to subdue
and discipline his masses of color by means of more clearly defined
forme. Now, a particular element—an oval or a circle—often became
the focus of the composition, and he frequently used the four-sided
figure of the trapezoid, and other geometric shapes laid diagonally
over the composition, to animate the pictorial surface and define the
subject of the painting.

IN THE GRAY, 1919. In works
like this, previously chaotic
compositions begin to become
more organized: the placement
of the two red areas and the
central black one announces
the artist's preference for
arranging forms along a
diagonal. Yet the black strokes
and threadlike lines are still
reminiscent of Kandinsky's
artistic idiom from the Munich
period.

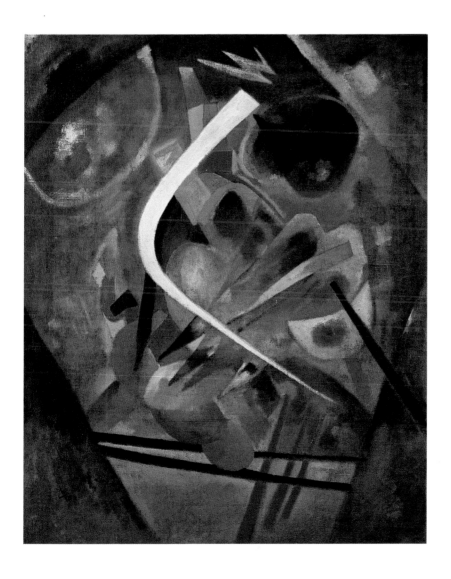

WHITE LINE, 1920. There is a
dynamic tension between the
rectangular shape of the canvas
itself and the large trapezoid
shape that seems to be in front
of it and whose corners extend
beyond the edges of the
painting. This two-layer effect,
together with the projecting
white arc in the middle, makes
the pictorial space seem to
bulge outward at the center, as
in a relief—a sharp difference
from the works of 1910 to 1914.

RED OVAL, 1920. The red oval
is a variation on the vortex
element familiar from
Kandinsky's earlier paintings,
but the large yellow plane that
organizes the picture as a
whole heralds a new,
increasingly geometric style.
Though the elements of
Kandinsky's vocabulary had
changed little since the Munich
period, he was composing with
them in a new way.

BLACK PATTERN, 1922. A trapezium
divided into tiny cells—to be
filled in with colors in later
paintings—here becomes the
center toward which the other
shapes gravitate. The geometri-
cally conceived forms are
arranged on overlapping planes.
The seeming evocation of ships
and fish in the lower left
corner is a touch of capricious
irony rather than a genuine
figurative reference.

POINT AND LINE TO PLANE

Kandinsky worked for eleven years—from 1922 to 1933—at the Bauhaus, first in Weimar and then in Dessau and Berlin. His experiences led him to systematize his practices as a painter into a body of teaching, most notably in the book *Point and Line to Plane,* published in 1926. The notion of musical and emotional equivalents to color, initially expounded in *On the Spiritual in Art,* continued to be at the core of his painting, but now this idea was combined with a new interaction of forms. Kandinsky had long pursued a theory of color based on an opposition between red and blue. With his increasing reliance on geometric shapes, he could use them to either intensify or reduce the inherent properties of each color, as well as mark directions and points of tension on the pictorial surface. He was careful, however, not to rely too heavily on theory, applying it freely, without falling into the trap of making painting the mechanical implementation of a formula.

COMPOSITION VIII, 1923. In this period of Kandinsky's career, the circle appears as a symbol of perfection, often carrying cosmic connotations. The vibrant color of the Blue Rider years is now applied more evenly and smoothly. The economy and exactitude of the geometric style establish a new sense of the absolute.

ON WHITE II, 1923. Two heavy black lines convey the twisting effect
created by the brown trapezoid as it tilts away from the picture
plane. The turning of the triangles and quadrilaterals in space
reflects this tension, and where they overlap there is a complex
mingling of their colors. For Kandinsky, the expressive character of
his art, its drama, arose from these dynamic interactions between
shapes and colors. "The encounter of a circle with the point of a
triangle," he wrote, "is no less affecting than God's finger
touching Adam's in the work of Michelangelo."

STILL TENSION, 1924. As the
title of this painting suggests,
its pictorial structure
demonstrates the balance between
opposing forces. The complex
interplay in the picture between
superimposed forms—a welter
of straight lines set against
curves and circles against
rectangles—is resolved by the
equilibrium between the two
principal circles, set in
opposite corners. The strong
diagonal axis that connects the
two is emphasized by an arrow.
The colors, too, are arranged
in accordance with this
opposition, so that the "warmer"
reds and yellows predominate
in the upper left and the
"cooler" blues in the lower
right. Within this color scheme,
the two circles serve as
alternatives: a cold vortex and
a hot one. The compositional
clarity sought in this type
of painting is a result both of
Kandinsky's evolution as an
artist and his concurrent
experience as a teacher.

HARD BUT SOFT, 1927. Once
again, the structural precision
is reminiscent of the work of
the Russian Constructivists.
The intricate network of straight
lines, circles, and triangles
generates a pattern of small,
separate cells, many of them
filled in with color. The title
suggests how the hardness of
this geometric structure is
played off against the softness
of the open, diaphanous
background.

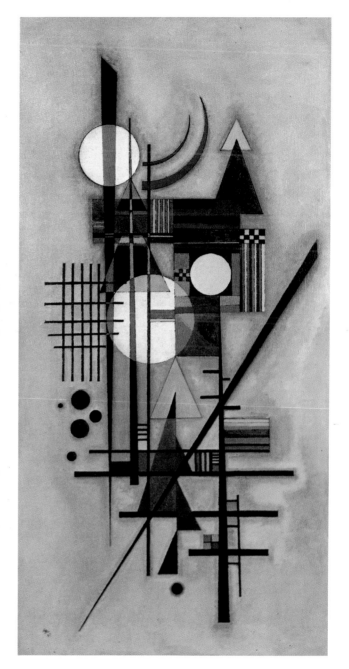

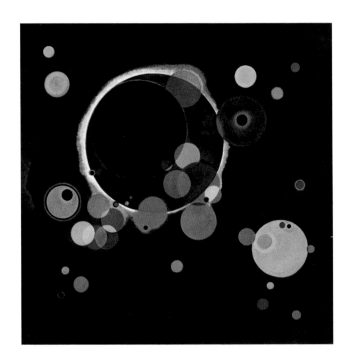

SEVERAL CIRCLES, 1926. Spheres and disks begin to appear in Kandinsky's work with the 1922 graphic portfolio *Little Worlds* (see p. 10), whereby he sought to reconcile the intellectual rigor of the Bauhaus with his own spiritualistic impulses. Thus, in one sense, geometric shapes such as the circle are the products of the rational mind, part of the system of mathematical measurement first developed by the ancient Greeks. Yet at the same time, as Kandinsky said, "a circle ... is a blazing patch of sky" —a solar disk, like the sun, endowed with cosmic overtones and thus a way of picturing, and understanding, the workings of the universe.

THIRTEEN RECTANGLES, 1930.
As if reversing the course
of his development, Kandinsky
seems to return to a kind
of rigor from which he was
actually more distant than he
may seem. This work may suggest
the Neoplasticist compositions
of Piet Mondrian and Theo van
Doesburg, but the staircase

arrangement of the rectangles,
which appears in a number of
paintings, also invokes an
occult notion of initiation and
spiritual progress. As in most
works from this period, the
entire composition is organized
around one element, in this
case the large, red square near
the center.

A NEW FREEDOM

Kandinsky's relation to European abstract painting after he settled in Paris in 1933 was not an easy one. Although, by that time, he was an established artist, his social circle in the French capital was rather restricted. In spite of that, however, his late works are characterized by the special freedom and tranquility sometimes seen in an artist's old age. Kandinsky abandoned the strict geometry that had distinguished the Bauhaus years and started practicing what can be called a "biomorphic" abstraction, on account of its softly organic, sinuous shapes. For some viewers, these images evoke the world revealed by the microscope, an association which may indeed have attracted the artist as an alternative to immediate perception, a fantastic universe concealed from the unaided senses. What the mysterious yet festive lyricism of these paintings really seeks, however, is the "inner gaze," that transcendental goal that Kandinsky had pursued throughout his career. In 1910, writing about the content of his paintings, he said that he wanted "to speak of secrets by means of a secret. Could this be the theme? Is this not the objective, conscious or unconscious, of the urgent creative impulse? With the language of art one can speak to humanity about what is beyond the human."

INTERRELATIONS, 1934. The small, dynamic, and brightly colored organic forms recall the appearance of protozoa, the tiny cells seen through the lens of a microscope. One cannot discount the influence of artists such as Jean Arp and Joan Miro, whom Kandinsky met during his years in Paris, but the principles governing the color relations remain the same as in his own previous works.

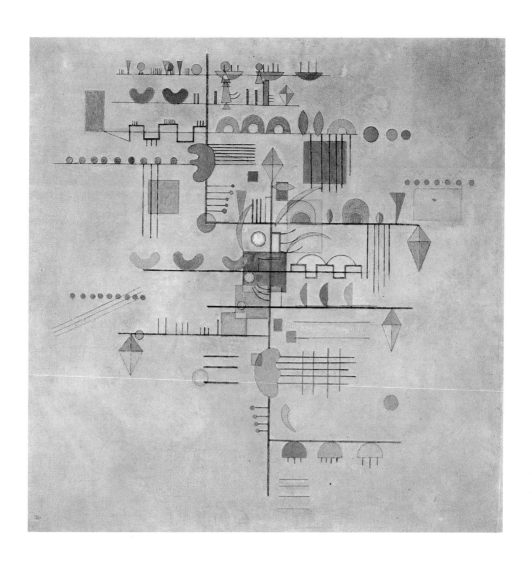

GRACEFUL ASCENT, 1934. The stepped arrangement of shapes seen in
Thirteen Rectangles (p. 65) returns here, but now it is presented
in a more uninhibited manner, like one of the miniature universes,
full of wit, devised by Paul Klee. The suggestion of a spiral,
created by the three small crescents above the central square,
subtly enhances the sense of upward movement, while also indicating
the kind of vortex that Kandinsky had employed in many of his
paintings since the Munich years

DOMINANT CURVE, 1936. The symbolic staircase, most evident at the lower right, here incorporates both geometric and organic forms. Though Kandinsky remained indebted to the compositional rigor of the Bauhaus, he also valued the greater freedom of the new idiom that he had now mastered.

ACCOMPANIED MILIEU, 1937. The familiar symbolism of the circle gives rise to myriad cur-vilinear shapes, the dominant one resembling the staff of a musical score, all set against a bright yellow field, like the gold background of an icon.

THE WHITE LINE, 1936. Kandinsky here makes use of the distinctively modernist whipping curve, so frequent, for instance, in the decorative works of August Endell, whom Kandinsky met during his first years in Munich. The biomorphic form under the white line, with its related indenting curves, evokes both the contours and the texture of a micro-organism, although recently it has been reinterpreted as a horse and rider.

UNANIMITY, 1939. One of the most distinctive features of Kandinsky's last phase is the progressive lightening of his palette, which often became extremely bright, as well as his greater use of blended hues, lessening the reliance on primary colors that had extended through the Munich and Bauhaus years.

COMPOSITION X, 1939. For
Kandinsky, abstraction
presupposed above all, the
creation of an autonomous
artistic universe, independent
of nature, and yet no less real
and concrete than the natural
world. The colored shapes
floating before a midnight
background tell of just such an
alternative and visionary
universe.

SKY BLUE, 1940. The biomorphic
forms seen here, looking like
fantastic animals, may refer to
the world of children's toys or
to that of Slavic folk art,
although Kandinsky was usually
vexed when critics made such
associations in talking about
his work.

ACCOMPANIED CONTRAST, 1935.
Generally not concerned with
purely technical innovation,
Kandinsky did nonetheless
sometimes experiment with using
sand to give texture to the
paint.

DELAYED ACTIONS, 1941. The
freedom and fluidity of
paintings such as this can make
for quite an elaborate
composition. A number of
segments throughout the picture
could easily have been developed
into paintings in their own
right. Indeed, many different
parts of the canvas carry equal
importance, without the focused
cores of tension typical of the
artist's earlier works.

CIRCLE AND SQUARE, 1943; THE SMALL RED CIRCLE, 1944. Kandinsky's
last works, of which these are two examples, display certain
devices from the geometric period, such as circles pierced by
triangles, or the interaction between straight lines and curves
generating the pictorial space. These are now presented in a
different context, of course, but the artist remains loyal to the
notion of an alternative painterly universe, only loosely connected
to the material world.

p 6
Moscow, Zubovsky Square III, c. 1916.
Oil on canvas, 34 × 32 cm.
Museum Ludwig, Cologne.

p 18
The Old City II, 1902.
Oil on canvas, 52 × 78.5 cm.
Musée National d'Art Moderne,
Centre Georges Pompidou, Paris.

p 19
Kochel: Waterfall I, 1900.
Oil on canvas over cardboard,
32.4 × 23.5 cm.
Städtische Galerie, Munich.

p 20
Riegsee: The Town Church, 1908.
Oil on cardboard, 33 × 45 cm.
Von der Heydt-Museum, Wuppertal.

p 21
**Munich: Schwabing with the Church
of St. Ursula,** 1908.
Oil on cardboard, 68.8 × 49 cm.
Städtische Galerie im Lenbachhaus,
Munich.

p 22
Landscape with a Tower, 1908.
Oil on cardboard, 74 × 98.5 cm.
Musée National d'Art Moderne,
Centre Georges Pompidou, Paris.

p 23
Interior (My Dining Room), 1909.
Oil on cardboard, 50 × 65 cm.
Städtische Galerie im Lenbachhaus,
Munich.

p 24
Mountain, 1909.
Oil on canvas, 109 × 109 cm.
Städtische Galerie im Lenbachhaus,
Munich.

p 25
Obermarkt with Mountains, 1908.
Oil on cardboard, 33 × 41 cm.
Private collection, Germany.

p 26
The Blue Rider, 1903.
Oil on canvas, 55 × 65 cm.
Private collection, Zurich.

p 27
Riding Couple, 1906–7.
Oil on canvas, 55 × 50.5 cm.
Städtische Galerie im Lenbachhaus,
Munich.

p 28
The Farewell, 1903.
Woodcut, 31.3 × 31.2 cm.
Musée National d'Art Moderne,
Centre Georges Pompidou, Paris.

p 29
Portrait of Gabriele Münter, 1905.
Oil on canvas, 45 × 45 cm.
Städtische Galerie im Lenbachhaus,
Munich.

p 30
Blue Mountain, 1908–9.
Oil on canvas, 106 × 96.6 cm.
Solomon R. Guggenheim Museum,
New York.

p 31
Murnau: The Garden I, 1910.
Oil on canvas, 66 × 82 cm.
Städtische Galerie im Lenbachhaus,
Munich.

p 32
**Murnau: View with Railroad and
Castle,** 1909.
Oil on cardboard, 36 × 49 cm.
Städtische Galerie im Lenbachhaus,
Munich.

p 33
Sketch for **Composition II,** 1910.
Oil on canvas, 97.5 × 131.2 cm.
Solomon R. Guggenheim Museum,
New York.

p 34
Improvisation VI, 1909.
Oil on canvas, 107 × 99.5 cm.
Städtische Galerie im Lenbachhaus,
Munich.

p 35
Improvisation VII, 1910.
Oil on canvas, 131 × 97 cm.
Tretyakov Gallery, Moscow.

p 36
**Improvisation XVIII (with
Tombstones),** 1911.
Oil on canvas, 141 × 120 cm.
Städtische Galerie im Lenbachhaus,
Munich.

p 37
Passage by Boat, 1910.
Oil on canvas, 98 × 105 cm.
Tretyakov Gallery, Moscow.

p 38
Improvisation XIX, 1911.
Oil on canvas, 120 × 141.5 cm.
Städtische Galerie im Lenbachhaus,
Munich.

p 39
All Saints' Day I, 1911.
Oil on cardboard, 50 × 64.5 cm.
Städtische Galerie im Lenbachhaus,
Munich.

p 40
Autumn II, 1912.
Oil on canvas, 60 × 82 cm.
The Phillips Collection, Washington, D.C.

p 41
Composition IV, 1911.
Oil on canvas, 159.5 × 250.5 cm.
Kunstsammlung Nordrhein-Westfalen,
Düsseldorf.

p 42
Improvisation XIII, 1910.
Oil on canvas, 120 × 140 cm.
Staatliche Kunsthalle, Karlsruhe.

p 43
St. George II, 1911.
Oil on canvas, 107 × 96 cm.
Russian Museum, St. Petersburg.

p 44
Deluge I, 1912.
Oil on canvas, 100 × 105 cm.
Kaiser-Wilhelm Museum, Krefeld.

p 45
Improvisation (Deluge), 1913.
Oil on canvas, 95 × 150 cm.
Städtische Galerie im Lenbachhaus,
Munich.

p 46
Study for **Deluge II,** 1912.
Oil on canvas, 95 × 107.5 cm.
Collection Harold Diamont, New
York.

p 47
Improvisation XXVI (Rowing), 1912.
Oil on canvas, 97 × 107.5 cm.
Städtische Galerie im Lenbachhaus,
Munich.

p 48
Composition VI, 1913.
Oil on canvas, 195 × 300 cm.
The State Hermitage Museum,
St. Petersburg.

p 49
Fantastic Improvisation, 1913.
Oil on canvas, 130 × 130 cm.
Städtische Galerie im Lenbachhaus,
Munich.

p 50
Moscow II, 1916.
Oil on canvas, 52 × 36 cm.
Private collection.

p 51
Black Lines I, 1913.
Oil on canvas, 129.4 × 131.1 cm.
Solomon R. Guggenheim Museum,
New York.

p 52
Song of the Volga, 1906.
Tempera on cardboard, 49 × 66 cm.
Musée National d'Art Moderne,
Centre Georges Pompidou, Paris.

p 53
Glass Painting with Sun, 1910.
Reverse painting on glass with
painted frame, 30.6 × 40.3 cm.
Städtische Galerie im Lenbachhaus,
Munich.

p 54
Last Judgment, 1912.
Reverse painting on glass with
painted frame, 33.6 × 45.3 cm.
Museé National d'Art Moderne,
Centre Georges Pompidou, Paris.

p 55
Woman in Moscow, 1912.
Oil on canvas, 108.8 × 108.8 cm.
Städtische Galerie im Lenbachhaus,
Munich.

p 56
In the Gray, 1919.
Oil on canvas, 129 × 176 cm.
Musée National d 'Art Moderne,
Centre Georges Pompidou, Paris.

p 57
White Line, 1920.
Oil on canvas, 98 × 80 cm.
Museum Ludwig, Cologne.

p 58
Red Oval, 1920.
Oil on canvas, 71.5 × 71.2 cm.
Solomon R. Guggenheim Museum,
New York.

p 59
Black Pattern, 1922.
Oil on canvas, 96 × 106 cm.
Musée National d'Art Moderne,
Centre Georges Pompidou, Paris.

p 60
Composition VIII, 1923.
Oil on canvas, 140 × 201 cm.
Solomon R. Guggenheim Museum,
New York.

p 61
On White II, 1923.
Oil on canvas, 105 × 98 cm.
Musée National d'Art Moderne,
Centre Georges Pompidou, Paris.

p 62
Still Tension, 1924.
Oil on cardboard, 78.5 × 54.5 cm.
Private collection, Paris.

p 63
Hard But Soft, 1927.
Oil on canvas,100 × 50 cm.
Museum of Fine Arts, Boston.

p 64
Several Circles, 1926.
Oil on canvas, 140 × 140 cm.
Solomon R. Guggenheim Museum,
New York.

p 65
Thirteen Rectangles, 1930.
Oil on cardboard, 69.5 × 59.5 cm.
Musée National d'Art Moderne,
Centrc Georges Pompidou, Paris.

p 66
Interrelations, 1934.
Mixed mediums on canvas,
89 × 116 cm.
Collection Mr. and Mrs. David Lloyd
Kreeger, Washington, D.C.

p 67
Graceful Ascent, 1934.
Oil on canvas, 80 × 80 cm.
Solomon R. Guggenheim Museum,
New York.

p 68
Dominant Curve, 1936.
Oil on canvas, 130 × 195 cm.
Solomon R. Guggenheim Museum,
New York.

p 69
Accompanied Milieu, 1937.
Oil on canvas, 114 × 146 cm.
Whereabouts unknown. Formerly
collection Adrien Maeght, Paris.

p 70
The White Line, 1936.
Gouache and tempera on black
paper, 49.9 × 38.7 cm.
Musée National d'Art Moderne,
Centre Georges Pompidou, Paris.

p 71
Unanimity, 1939.
Oil on canvas, 73 × 92 cm.
Collection Jeffrey H. Loria, New York.

p 72
Composition X, 1939.
Oil on canvas, 130 × 195 cm.
Kunstsammlung Nordrhein-Westfalen,
Düsseldorf.

p 73
Sky Blue, 1940.
Oil on canvas, 100 × 73 cm.
Musée National d'Art Moderne,
Centre Georges Pompidou, Paris.

p 74
Accompanied Contrast, 1935.
Oil with sand on canvas, 97 × 162 cm.
Solomon R. Guggenheim Museum,
New York.

p 75
Delayed Actions, 1941.
Mixed mediums on canvas,
89 × 116 cm.
Solomon R. Guggenheim Museum,
New York.

p 76
Circle and Square, 1943.
Tempera and oil on cardboard,
42 × 58 cm.
Musée Natioٮal d'Art Moderne,
Centre Georges Pompidou, Paris.

p 77
The Small Red Circle, 1944.
Gouache and oil on cardboard,
42 × 58 cm.
Musée National d'Art Moderne,
Centre Georges Pompidou, Paris.

SELECTED BIBLIOGRAPHY

Avtonomova, Natalia, Vivian Endicott
Barnett, et al. *New Perspectives on
Kandinsky.* Malmö, Sweden: Malmö
Konsthall, Sydsvenska Dagbladet,
1990.

Dabrowski, Magdalena. *Kandinsky:
Compositions.* New York: The
Museum of Modern Art, 1995.

Grohmann, Will. *Wassily Kandinsky:
Life and Work.* New York: Harry N.
Abrams, Inc., 1958.

Hahl-Koch, Jelena. *Kandinsky.* New
York: Rizzoli, 1993.

Lindsay, Kenneth C., and Peter Vergo,
eds. *Kandinsky: Complete Writings
on Art.* Rev. ed., New York: Da Capo
Press, 1994.

Roethel, Hans K., and Jean K.
Benjamin. *Kandinsky: Catalogue
Raisonne of the Oil Paintings.* 2 vols.
Ithaca, N.Y.: Cornell University Press,
1982, 1984.

Washton Long, Rose-Carol. *Kandinsky:
The Development of an Abstract
Style.* Oxford: Clarendon Press, 1980.

Weiss, Peg. *Kandinsky and "Old
Russia": The Artist as Ethnographer
and Shaman.* New Haven, Conn.,
and London: Yale University Press,
1995.